Monument
to a
Black Man

William Goyens —
    His skin was black;
        His heart, true blue.

Monument to a Black Man

by Daniel James Kubiak

Illustrations by Neil Caldwell

The Naylor Company
Book Publishers of the Southwest
San Antonio, Texas

Also by the author:
Ten Tall Texans

Library of Congress Cataloging in Publication Data

Kubiak, Daniel James.
Monument to a Black man.

Bibliography: p.
1. Goyens, William, 1794-1856. I. Title.
E185.97.G68K8   976.4'03'0924   [B]   72-5102
ISBN 0-8111-0440-0

"He well knows what snares are spread about his path, from personal animosity . . . and possibly from popular delusion. But he has put to hazard his ease, his security, his interest, his power, even his . . . popularity. . . . He is traduced and abused for his supposed motives. He will remember that obloquy is a necessary ingredient in the composition of all true glory: he will remember . . . that calumny and abuse are essential parts of triumph. . . . He may live long, he may do much. But here is the summit. He never can exceed what he does this day."

— Edmund Burke's eulogy of Charles James Fox for his attack upon the tyranny of the East India Company. House of Commons, December 1, 1783.

Preface

THIS BOOK,
the first in the comprehensive biographical study of
William Goyens on which I have long engaged, covers
his entire lifetime and is a unit in itself. It has been
virtually complete for over a year, but was withheld
because of my desire to finish the study of the entire
life of the great Negro leader, an individual who, in
the early days of Texas, contributed so much toward
helping bring peace to a troubled Republic. At this
writing, my work has advanced to the point where
I feel warranted in releasing this account of William
Goyens.

I have learned much concerning this individual
from documents, from theses, from dissertations, and
from letters which have been written and stored in

libraries throughout Texas and throughout the southern part of the United States. I feel relatively safe in promising that, barring accidents, material covering the lapse of time between various incidents in this book will someday be found. It is my hope that this account of the great free Negro in the Texas frontier will be such that it will instill pride in all Americans in the contributions that one Negro leader made during a troubled period in American history when slavery was prevalent throughout the United States.

On turning back the leaves of the calendar, I am dismayed by the discovery that I have been unable to proceed through William Goyens' life as an investigator and writer any faster than he himself did as a living man. I have met with a number of unforeseen interruptions, but my main difficulties have arisen from the very nature of the task. In writing this book, I have referred to many documents, and was especially pleased with the document written by a young lady, Miss Diane Elizabeth Prince who, in her thesis presented to the faculty of the graduate school of Stephen F. Austin State College, did much research into this man's life. I owe a great deal to the Library of Congress for the tremendous amount of aid they presented throughout my search for information concerning William Goyens. There are many others to be mentioned — the libraries in Texas and those in North and South Carolina — I am grateful to all of these for the help that they presented.

William Goyens was an individual whose entire life was a complicated part of his career, and the materials bearing on it are considerably more extensive than in any other area of anyone's life during this period. During his lifetime, William Goyens merged with the history of his country in being a leader, not only for his race but for all the people. He was to be related to far more events and persons even though he was a smaller man, a lesser man, and even a slave in the East.

He was above battle, he was above fear, he was a man dedicated to a cause, for he was a great individual and was to be a private man. He received communications about public affairs by every post, and only when riding on horseback about his farms near Nacogdoches or tinkering with some gadget or enjoying the companionship of some fellowman could he be oblivious of what was going on in Texas, in the Republic, and in the United States.

Anyone who aspires to write the biography of a man, and especially one of a minority group, must familiarize himself as best he can with the major events and developments in the country as a whole, and in dealing with an age when international relations were of prime importance to Texas as a Mexican province, and later as a Republic, should try to see things in a world setting. It is difficult to realize that the Negro at that time had no freedom, but was a slave, and it was during this period that William Goyens grew in greatness and became a great leader for his people.

In trying to establish all these things, it was my first concern to determine and to report accurately what happened and how it happened. With the passing of time, the downright misrepresentations that gather around an eminent and very highly controversial public figure are difficult and exacting, but no one who would tell a true and honest story can escape this. In the course of this book, I frequently point out what I regard as mistakes and misjudgments by William

Goyens' contemporaries, but my general policy has been to let the facts as I have ascertained them speak for themselves. It is my hope that all of these facts are true and accurate, and they are to the best of my ability.

It is not easy to trace an individual's life, for the facts are limited and are sparsely scattered. While I am much indebted to certain monographs and have greatly benefitted from the labors of other scholars, this is a fresh study based on original sources, and it must stand on its own. The biographer or historian, besides trying to answer the questions what and how, should do everything he can to find out why things happened in his effort to arrive at the fullest possible understanding, and should not subject himself to the charge of trying to explain things away. I hope this work constitutes a contribution to knowledge, but knowledge can avail little if it does not contribute to understanding.

The difficulty of reading the minds of men, great in any case, is magnified in light of the many sides of William Goyens, who was an individual as complicated as any who has ever lived. It is not at all surprising that his aims and motives have been variously interpreted. There is something in him for almost everyone whether we be Negroid, Mongoloid, or Caucasoid, and through the years the tendency has been for observers to see in him what they wanted to see. This is especially true of those whose interest in him has been primarily political.

Without claiming to have arrived at the whole truth about him as a public man, I shall venture some reflections on the relations between his political ideas and the contributions that he made to Texas, to the

Republic, to Sam Houston, and to those with whom he dealt throughout America. He is an individual who shall not be forgotten, but delving into this book, you will find many areas which apply so much to this day and time.

This man was not affected because of his race. He did not let his color bother his full development. He reacted against those who opposed him and against despotism that marked the period. Though he was less disillusioned with his countrymen than were his friends, he came out of the country during the most critical years, and was less disturbed than they by the domestic turmoil and was more fearful of the hypocrisy that he had observed firsthand in South and North Carolina. He certainly viewed the aftermath of the Texas Revolution with none of the dismay and distaste that many had for the Mexican who lived in Texas at that time.

He was an individual, shrewd in his dealings, and with a dignity that any great man would have. He faced fear, he met the challenges of his day, and he himself undoubtedly regarded his victory as a vindication of the slavery that existed in the United States until after the Civil War.

He was not above voicing clichés for political purposes, but beyond any doubt, he was convinced that there was a place in Texas for a mulatto, as he was called in the time when slavery was prominent throughout the South. Unquestionably he intended, by his dedication to America in fighting in the War of 1812, to reaffirm the truth that was proclaimed so eloquently in the Declaration of Independence and the Bill of Rights for establishing religious freedom in America. He regarded these truths as self-evident and immutable. As for the doctrine of the sovereignty of the people in the American context, this was so fundamental that virtually everyone paid it lip service, but William Goyens was a man who had a difference of opinion and respected the individual's rights. He became a wealthy man with reliance on the common people generally and notably throughout his career, but he was well aware of his limitations, because he was a Negro at a time when the Negro was, supposedly, a second-class citizen. He faced many dangers, and he fully recognized that, except in a small locality, he would be an individual who would be discriminated against. Not once did he step down nor did he step aside whenever he knew that his conscience and convictions were true.

He welcomed opportunities, and he believed in using his talents and his virtues. As an aide to Sam Houston, he was concerned for efficiency in dealing with the Indians in trying to work out the many problems between the red man and the white man. He was never an indiscriminating person, but, clearly, was more democratic than anyone in his area during the early 1800s. He was a man of the people who never stepped out of line for the sake of demonstrating, but was a man who was accorded by many followers as a true American. In looking further into the life of William Goyens, we find other areas in which he was consistently respectful of his fellowman. He called upon many Anglos to help in this way in and around Nacogdoches. He exercised influence on legislation during those early years, and the circumstances under which he did this are described in various chapters throughout the book. He learned at an early age that he must rely on his own abilities and his own initiative in order to succeed in this new country. He clearly recognized that he would be somewhat handicapped, but never once allowed the cynics, the critics, who were sometimes devious, secretive, and hypercritical, to overcome him. He was a man who was tactful, discreet, and modest.

It seems clear that in the climate of opinion in those circumstances he followed the course that was likely to be most fruitful and acceptable. He may have had some qualms, but the results demonstrated the political sanctity. This was a man who set his views on the proper relationship between the independent man of his time and those condemned to slavery. It seems difficult to truly evaluate William Goyens as he was, for he was an individual who today can be looked upon as a great Texan and a great American. His popularity in Nacogdoches and in East Texas was probably due primarily to his policies, for he believed in doing unto others as he would have them do unto him, and he himself symbolized freedom and democracy. His personal contacts with the citizenry were necessarily very limited, but in those he had, he showed clearly his respect for the dignity of personality and individualism. There is a good deal about him as a person in this book, especially in the sections so marked. He did not cease to be a devoted man, a dedicated man, and he was saddened somewhat when people attempted to take advantage of him. He was a man who exhibited a love of country, a fear of God, and a greatness which all of us possess to some degree. He has been viewed by some as a man of paradox whose contradictions cannot be resolved. I would not seek to rob him of his fascination by reducing him to a dull level of uniformity, but few things about him have impressed me more than his extraordinary ability to hold diverse and even contradictory things in equilibrium. He was a man in whom I feel you will be interested and with whom you will want to become more familiar. It is an honor and a privilege to bring you my second book, a book entitled, *Monument to a Black Man.*

Daniel James Kubiak

Acknowledgements

I WOULD LIKE to express my appreciation to State Representative Neil Caldwell of Alvin for his artistic renditions used extensively throughout *Monument to a Black Man.* His personal contributions added significantly to the contents of this book.

Grace Curtis and Peggy Hosek of Rockdale deserve special thanks for their untiring efforts in helping me compile, assemble and complete this, my second book. Without their help and cooperation throughout the writing and final publication of *Monument to a Black Man,* this could not have been possible.

My sincere appreciation to Miss Elizabeth Prince whose master's thesis at Stephen F. Austin University inspired me to write *Monument to a Black Man.* Her research and efforts aided me tremendously in my quest for specific facts concerning Will Goyens.

And finally, I want to express my sincerest appreciation to my wife, Zana, and to my son, Kelly Dan, whose patience and understanding aided me so much in compiling the story of Will Goyens.

My sincere appreciation to my parents, to those teachers, faculty members, colleagues in the Texas Legislature, students and friends who have through life aided me in my endeavors. I am, and forever shall be, grateful. For I am a part of all that I have met and seen.

DANIEL JAMES KUBIAK

1

IT WAS BECOMING
more difficult to breathe as the hours passed. It seemed
like yesterday when he had been a young man, but
the hour of calling was upon him, and he knew it was
calling William Goyens. Death was then the item that
called the man who had done so much for his people
at a time when his people were considered slaves in all
of America, the land of the free. During the decade of
the 1850s, the slavery issue reached a critical stage,
and the status of the free Negro became increasingly
precarious. Conditions in the recently admitted slave
State of Texas were certainly no exception. Indeed,
more discrimination was reflected in the attitude of
the white population and in the attitude of the government.

1

Three hundred and ninety-seven free Negroes of Texas in 1850[1] must surely have watched with great interest the debates across the nation over the extension of slavery into the territories. William Goyens and his wife did not see the final outcome of this particular question. Both died in 1856 at the height of the controversies over Kansas' personal liberty laws, and slavery extension. This was the way that a great man, a great free Negro had lived and then died.

The sight of men losing their freedom was an ordinary thing in the year of 1815 and had been all of the life of William Goyens; yet many men including Sam Houston remarked, "I would rather have lost the best man in my power than to have lost a counselor as William Goyens." He was sixty-two years of age when he succumbed in Nacogdoches. Respected for goodness and wisdom, learning and wit, he was a statesman for Texas. A patriot in every sense, Goyens never received a high office. He was a man who was dedicated to helping others throughout his lifetime. He was a black man; yet he believed that all men are created equal and that in this country a man could set aside his color, forget his many obstacles, and in turn, dedicate his life to the constitutional principle that all men are created equal.

He was a friend of Sam Houston and had been his confidant. Houston was so impressed with Goyens that he gave him all the duties of securing the treaties with the Indians. Goyens was one of the largest landowners in the territory, and he was a free man at a time when a Negro was not to be free; but he had

---

[1] The census figures on the free Negroes may not be completely reliable since Mexicans were sometimes possibly mistaken as mulattoes.

2

done this in a manner of circumstance that his conduct was characterized by humility and calmness of spirit which did not desert him even on his dying bed. He was then calm enough to jest with those about him, humble enough to accept the prayers of all concerned. "Splendid and triumphant," was his final utterance; then he died, the servant of all mankind.

He had the vision of a great reformer, and he possessed the genius to translate his hopes and dreams into an understanding form and pattern. He yearned for a better world for all men, not just the Negro people.

Goyens was one of the first victims of land fraud and scandalous affairs. Though not unique, these were engineered for and by the privileged. On his dying day, a voucher appeared against the Goyens' estate presented by one George Clevenger. From this, one can approximate the date of his wife's death. Several items were charged to Goyens by Clevenger in that month for materials such as lumber, a shovel, and spades which most likely had been used for her burial. These were the things which Goyens had provided so that he in turn would not be a burden on any man.

Goyens became ill at his home in June of the year 1856, but he had been active in his business affairs as late as January 17, 1856. On that day he sold one hundred acres of land, located eight miles southwest from the town of Nacogdoches near the Alazan Creek, to Alexander Myers, and another one hundred acres to Thomas J. Collins, both at $1.50 per acre. No business transactions were recorded except personal purchases between that date and the day of his untimely death.

In accounts about this great free Negro, we learn that Dr. William Tubbe was in attendance on Goyens for three days and four nights before Goyens' life was terminated on that fateful June 20, 1856. He was buried beside his wife near a large cedar tree on Moral Creek in a Mexican cemetery approximately three miles from his home. The following year a fence was placed around the graves of William Goyens and his faithful wife.

Sam Houston described William Goyens as "one of the greatest persons of integrity known to Texas during the 1800s." He was paid tribute by Anglo and Negro alike who knew of his many endeavors. He was coming into his own as a major prophet of social progress and he was an individual who would be studied by many for generations to come.

The State of Texas in 1936, sensing Goyens' historical significance, placed a historical marker near the site of the grave making him the only Negro to be so recognized. The marker on the grave of William Goyens, five miles west of Nacogdoches, contains several errors as research later proved. First, he was born free, not a slave; in North Carolina, not South Carolina; and died in 1856, not 1836.[2] This was the man whose dedication to duty speaks more eloquently than any other single element. Nothing shows more distinctly how he towered above his contemporaries, but it required more than a hundred years before the conditions existed which enabled anyone to perceive

---

2 The marker reads as follows, "William ('Bill') Goyens, born a slave in South Carolina, 1794. Escaped to Texas in 1821. Rendered valuable assistance to the Army of Texas, 1836. Interpreter for the Houston-Forbes Treaty with the Cherokees, 1836. Acquired wealth and was noted for his charity. Died at his home on Goyens Hill 1836. His skin was black; his heart, true blue."

4

The marker on the grave of William Goyens, five miles west of Nacogdoches, contains several errors as research later proved.

how Goyens set himself apart from many of the prejudices that beset his race. He did not sit idly dreaming in a leisure hour, but had profound insight into the essentials and of the necessities of his age. Although gone for over a century, the ideals of William Goyens are not vanquished, but are still alive before a striving mankind today.

2

WILLIAM GOYENS WAS BORN in 1794 just a few short years after the American Revolution. Although not of noble rank, the families of his parents were neverthless people who knew their sons and daughters must have compassion, must be helpful, and must do whatever they could to upgrade mankind. His father reared nine children in Moore County, North Carolina, in the Fayetteville district. At an early age, all members of this family were described as "not white" in the census, which indicated that all references to William Goyens and his family were as mulattoes.

Throughout the records Goyens was spoken of as being a mulatto or light Negro. Apparently he was lighter than most mulattoes since he was a quadroon. It was a petition from the district court in Carthage, Moore County, North Carolina, in 1845 that substantiated that John M. Goyens was a free man of good character. The document states that he was born and brought up in this county, was now a citizen thereof at the age of twenty-seven years, that his grandfather, William Goyens, Sr. was a respectable citizen of this county, not of altogether white complexion, but also a free man, and exercised the privileges as such while he lived. The grandmother was a free white woman, the daughter Leah was the mother of the petitioner. There was only one William Goyens, (Sr.) mulatto, in the North Carolina census of 1790. Therefore, considering the ages, Leah was William Goyens, Jr.'s sister and John M. Goyens, his nephew.

In the colorful story of North Carolina there seldom has been a more vivid period than that period of the 1790s. The passing of the eighteenth century, the coming of the nineteenth, presented a pageant which was reflected in the turbulent streets of America itself. The rich dress — the merchants — the rich individuals — the nobles — were what William Goyens watched as a young man in North Carolina. This he never had, but his father fitted well into the time and the place. William Goyens, Sr. liked life and lived it fully; a man who was intelligent, shrewd, and very witty. Commenting upon the hazards of matrimony, he compared the multitude of women who were chosen for wives to "a bagful of snakes and eels together, seven snakes for one eel." He was a man who reared nine children, but his most famous was William Goyens, Jr.

It was during these formative years that William

Goyens, Jr. understood fully what it meant to be born a Negro in a state where Negroes were slaves. He had no basic freedoms and he was cautious in all that he said, in all that he did. It was not wise for a man who was not of the Anglo descent to even attempt any type of endeavor in North Carolina. Many things happened during his childhood which left an imprint on him. Many things he would recall, for these were the formative years, the years that would make him the great man that he was destined to become. He was sincere and this he learned from his father. He was taught never to deceive lest he be deceived himself. He did not forget, and this was the one thing which earned him the respect of all who came in contact with him.

Throughout his early life in North Carolina, he tried to watch the Anglo, yet he did not understand why he himself did not have the same privileges that were extended to the white race far and near. He would stand back in the shadows and watch, for he was not accepted in any crowd in any part of North Carolina. His ambition and goal in life was to be treated as a free man, to be able to own property, to be able to have some dignity as an individual in the country where there was supposed to be the guarantee of freedom and democracy.

In his childhood years, he played with many Anglo children in the counties in North Carolina, and he found that the only way he would receive an education was to attempt to read books. William Goyens did learn to read, and he learned it at an early age. Books were scarce, but he would borrow here and there from the masters who dominated the many plantations of North Carolina.

He was a studious and charitable leader among many of his Anglo friends. One of his very dear friends predicted early in life that he was no ordinary man, that he was no slave. He was an individual who would someday change the lives of so many who would follow him.

He was approximately twelve years old when he had his first dazzling experience in the shadow of many politicians, petitioners, and churchmen. Goyens asked his dear friend what he could do to become one of them. The reply, "Nothing, you are a black man, and nothing you will ever do can change that. Go to Mexico, Goyens. There you may have a chance in life. Here you will never amount to much more than a slave." It was he who stood as a coachman beside his master to do whatever was necessary. People observed that he had a wonderful stature and that he was gentle in communication, yet earnest and sincere. He had delightful experiences many times, but fun without harm to any of his fellow beings. There was no way in North Carolina, however, that he could ever rise above his environment. He was a man who was branded as inferior unless he could make the most of the circumstances that surrounded him.

Inspired by the spirit of humanism, Goyens decided to leave his beloved North Carolina someday for a state or a place where he would be given an equal opportunity to prove that he was just as good a man as any who existed. He studied, he read, he learned, and became a remarkable scholar. Goyens mastered rhetoric and logic, and stood above many of his friends who sometimes became enraged because of Goyens' knowledge of the various books. He performed and learned well. He listened to the many

10

men who gathered in the town square and took many of their ideas to heart. Goyens indulged in no vice or vain pleasures. He spent no time in idle pastimes, but did the best he could to enlighten himself so that poverty would not prevent him from being happy.

William Goyens loved the beauty of North Carolina, the landscape, the comfort and comradeship that he received. His family was poor as he had eight brothers and sisters, but this never seemed to bother the young Goyens for he was not bent by the power of wealth. Instead he turned to books so that his knowledge would remain with him through the many years. Goyens had no formal education, but in many ways gained even more because of his tremendous desire to learn.

As he grew older, he heard tales of a place called Texas, but it seemed so far away. Many times he dreamed of this distant land, and even had motives to leave, but none were very strong. After years of setbacks and the inability to get ahead, William Goyens' strongest motive for moving to Texas was to leave the stifled life of a free Negro in the South. Free Negroes in North Carolina like William Goyens found themselves in a position like that of others in their caste throughout the South. One North Carolina law affected the free person of color. This provided that all Negroes, Indians, mulattoes, and all persons of mixed blood descending from Negro in any ancestors, to the fourth generation inclusive, be restricted from being a free man or woman. The North Carolina law and the southern attitudes reflected and represented the situation in the first two decades of the nineteenth century.

There was also a law passed in 1741 placing a

fine on anyone participating in any type of mixed marriages. This was something which would always haunt the free Negro, William Goyens. He was free only because his father had fought in the Revolutionary War. His father played an important role for without the aid of the Negro slaves, there was no way that freedom could have become a reality for the Americans.

William Goyens was proud of his father. He had been told how, during the American Revolution the North Carolinians felt so threatened by the British at one particular point of the conflict, her assembly promised freedom to any slave serving in the army. William Goyens also remembered how his father in the years to follow elaborated on many of those conflicts with the British. All of these things, however, did not help William Goyens for he was branded a slave in North Carolina.

Some of his North Carolina friends had left for Texas. Through letters they shared their interests with William Goyens and assured him that there were lands to the west where a man could be free. They told him how Texas was rich and that it had a great history of many men of varied interests and talents, men who helped shape her into a great territory. Goyens read parts of the early Texas history and learned of the varied origins and races of people who made up this new territory. Here was a land that offered opportunity to a free Negro, so to Texas William Goyens decided to go.

William Goyens' father was one of approximately 5,000 Negroes who fought for America's independence in the Revolutionary War.

3

WILLIAM GOYENS' FATHER
resented the idea of his son going to Texas, being so
far removed from the family and from his homeland.
The senior Goyens was a man of common sense who
had arranged and set the path of a safe and prosperous
living for his son. He was proud of the progress William Goyens, Jr. made in all that he attempted, and he
could not understand the other diversion. The father
considered going to Texas a waste of time and a danger
to his own plan. An argument arose between father
and son and, in an attempt to uphold parental authority, the father reduced the small allowance that William Goyens had received. The senior Goyens was not
mistaken in thinking that his plans for his son's career

15

in North Carolina were in danger, for his son was a levelheaded young man. William Goyens was well educated through his own efforts, but Texas beckoned and had a great influence on his life during these formative years. He had no choice but to strike out for Texas, to try his luck in building his future.

The eighteenth century was relatively young when Goyens departed from North Carolina. During the next two years Goyens established a permanent residence in Texas near the town of Nacogdoches. He was to remain a resident near Nacogdoches during the Mexican era, the Texas Revolution, the years of the Republic, and the early years of statehood. It was on September 1, 1824 that the first record was made of William Goyens' residence in Texas. Anyone who knew William Goyens was not surprised that he was on the voting list for the election of an alcalde in Nacogdoches. He had been in Texas four years, since he had first stepped on Texas soil in 1820.

In Texas William Goyens found that he did not have to wear a piece of cloth on the left shoulder which said "free" as he had to do in some towns in North Carolina. There he had been identified by a patch and this established him as a free man. Other basic laws in North Carolina were not good for a free Negro and forced him into an extremely limited social and economic life.

William Goyens remembered the early and pre-Civil War South when men were living in a state of limbo. He was neither slave nor equal to the white man under the law or in the minds of the citizens of North Carolina, and the other southern states. Though he had escaped the harshness of slavery and had enjoyed some privileges under the law, he always found

16

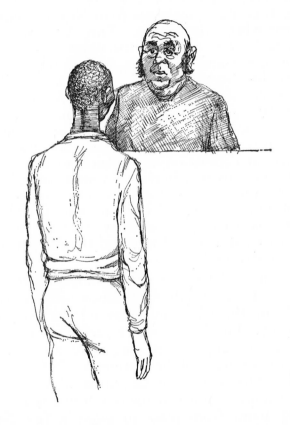

"A free African population is a curse to any country. Nature's God intended the African for the status of slavery."

laws across the South that restricted his life in many ways. Goyens remembered the slave owners in the South. They viewed the free Negro as a threat to slavery since slaves could see freed Negroes going and working where they pleased. This, William Goyens knew, had a bad effect on the slaves, for they were human beings and they, too, wanted their freedom. The Anglos also knew that the free Negro would have to be an ally of his brothers who were slaves.

As William Goyens stood on Texas soil near Nacogdoches, he recalled an antebellum judge from South Carolina who had personally told him that a free African population was a curse to any country. William Goyens was hurt and would remember this statement always. Laws throughout the South involving the free Negroes reflected the general view that these people were an irregularity, a living contradiction, "that nature's God intended the African for the status of slavery."

In contemplating his past, William Goyens cited the great James Madison. Madison felt the general attitude of the white man toward the Negro was derogatory. The Negro was regarded as a nuisance who must remain such as long as he was under the degradation which public sentiment inflicted on him. A great writer, as William Goyens recalled, stated that the prevailing attitude in the South was that . . . in moving about from place to place, a free Negro's right to liberties was always subject to question by whites. The mantle of suspicion was always around him. Regardless of how long the individual had been accepted as a free Negro in the community in which he lived, there was always the possibility that descendants of his former master or of his ancestor's master might attempt to force him back into slavery.

In North Carolina Goyens was not permitted to carry firearms or to buy or sell liquor. Stiff penalties were imposed on Negroes while lesser penalties for the same crime were imposed on white people. William Goyens went to the various places in North Carolina with high purposes and hopes, he recalled. He lived as an ordinary Negro, had no riches, and was given a pallet in a house which had four bare walls. In the wintertime, these walls permitted the cold wind to keep the temperature inside equal to that outside.

According to the family tradition recorded by his great-grandfather, William Goyens tried to pattern his life after a singular layman, Capt. John Smith whose biography he had studied in early life. Goyens translated the book and studied it diligently for this was a man who had both character and courage. Goyens had been endowed with high intellect and personal charm and had a desire to be successful. He was fascinated by philosophy and theology.

The early 1800s brought rogues as well as saints to North Carolina, and there must have been many in the state who did not take their lives as seriously as Goyens. In a structure with a dominating dollar and positions that were often held by ruthless men, the same opportunities were not offered to the Negro man. William Goyens disavowed many of the actions of those around him, but did so quietly. Goyens had to be careful for North Carolina was no place for a free Negro to succeed, and he was a creature of ambition. For the true aesthetic, and this Goyens was, it was a sacrifice to leave the tranquility of North Carolina and to reject the life that was offered to him there.

19

One questions why William Goyens so suddenly and so ardently became the busy man and the servant of mankind. Was the long self-examination of his youth a deliberate test to determine his allegiance to the Negro race and to mankind? Was this an effort to ascertain whether he was better suited to serve North Carolina or the great State of Texas? He was warned early in life by one of his subordinates, he recalled, "You ought anxiously to consider again and again what sort of burden this is which you are taking upon yourself of your own accord. Up to this you are free. You may still be if you choose. Turn to the aims and desires of North Carolina."

Still another friend was of the opinion that it was a question of free man versus slavery which turned Goyens to Texas. "When of a sentimental age, he was not a stranger to the emotions of people but without loss of character, having no inclination to press his advantage and being more attracted to Texas than any other place. He applied his whole mind to going to Texas having some thought of taking with him only the essentials. He had prepared himself by reading, by studying, and doing that which was necessary to gain wisdom. To know people was William Goyens' desire, but he could not shake off his wish to be truly a free man. Accordingly, he resolved to be a free man rather than a slave the rest of his life."

In support of his friends' statement that Goyens was not a stranger to the needs of mankind, there is a poem that was written in later years dedicated to the thoughts of William Goyens. The poem read as follows,

Severed, our different fates we then pursued,
   Till this late date our raptures have renewed.

Crimeless, my heart you stole in life's soft prime,
    and still possesses that heart without a crime.
Pure was the love which in my youth prevailed
    In age would keep it pure, if honor failed.
For may the Gods who five long lustres past,
    Have brought us to each other, well at last.
Grant that when numbered five long lustres more,
    Healthful I still may hail thee healthful as before.

William Goyens wanted to be a free man rather than a slave. Once having decided this, Goyens lost no time in preparing himself for it in faraway Texas. In working he hated to leave his many friends in North Carolina, and as a result found it hard to depart. All of the rigid requirements and regulations not only in North Carolina, but in the eastern United States, gave William Goyens and other free Negroes the incentive to flee to an area where they could have equal opportunities. By fleeing to a new land, Goyens later proved to be a valuable member of society and a man who would protect his liberty when all else failed.

The role of a free man benefitted William Goyens awkwardly at the beginning, for he was not used to having this type of free life. He missed the companionship of his brothers and sisters and disliked the exchange of the rustic peace for the Texas journey. From childhood his companions had been elderly and serious individuals, and it is true that there was this lighter side to his nature, for he was a man of broad humor and later kept a clown in his house in the way of making himself laugh when all things around him seemed bleak. The many heavy excursions into philosophy and even into theology provided much for the man who was to evolve. He had come to Texas, and he was standing here on soil which would soon take

21

him up. His adjustment would not come easy, for whatever the reason, the adjustment to a new land would be a difficult one. These were the years which would change his life and would make him the man of Texas.

Goyens liked this new land, this new soil and this new scenery, for Mexico placed no restrictions on the lives of Negroes in her colonies, and it was here in the Mexican borderlands that Goyens found an asylum, a place of retreat for free persons of color. For Goyens this was the Mexican west, and it held the key to his freedom, his dignity and his security. This area, the glorious part of the North American continent, was a section where every man could depend upon his ability and his convictions.

4

HE HAD COME BY SEA
to New Orleans and then overland to Texas and
arrived there in 1820. An article in the *Galveston
Daily News* written in 1904 by H. C. Fuller stated
things which were very pertinent concerning William
Goyens. Although his account of Goyens is full of
mistakes and inconsistencies, Fuller presented an account of Goyens that cannot be ignored.

In Texas, William Goyens joined the Anglo-
Americans who had come here by way of El Camino
Real from Natchitoches, Louisiana, to Nacogdoches,
which was considered the port of entry to the Spanish
territory. This route took the adventurous William
Goyens through thick woods, the low wet Sabine

River bottom to the rolling pine covered hills of the beautiful East Texas area. Between Natchitoches and Nacogdoches, there were a few scattered farms in 1820, but from Nacogdoches along the El Camino Real to San Antonio de Bexar, there was only wilderness.

Goyens looked around the ground which he had visited. In 1820 Nacogdoches was the only town in East Texas of any size whatsoever. Most pioneers settled there. San Augustine had not taken on the proportions of a town, and San Antonio to the south was only a way station. Like all others — the East Texas Indians, the Spanish and the French missionaries, the soldiers — William Goyens travelled this road to Nacogdoches.

By 1820, the Anglo-American settlers searched, as did Goyens, for the new life in Texas. The immigrants came for varied reasons: land and economic betterment, escape from the obligations of death under law, a new beginning in a new area of what was later to become the United States and, most of all, for adventure.

When arriving in Texas, William Goyens undoubtedly heard talk of many of the important events, and each of these was exciting to the free Negro in a free world. Goyens heard stories of Sam Houston, the man who later rose to lead the Texans and who was to become a close ally of William Goyens and who was a newcomer to Texas during this period. He also heard stories of Long's Rebellion. This publicity greatly influenced the recently immigrated free Negro to stay in Nacogdoches. Indian warfare, the Mexican Revolution and even Long's Rebellion left Nacogdoches in ruins, and most of the residents fled into Louisiana

This new land offered opportunities for excitement and adventure, but most important, it offered freedom for every individual.

crossing the Sabine River. It was Stephen F. Austin who, in the year 1821, recorded in his diary that Nacogdoches lay in ruins, with only a church still standing in what once was a flourishing settlement.

In all of this, nothing stopped William Goyens from succeeding in a new part of the world. The population continued to grow, and the Mexican government passed a colonization law on January 4, 1823 encouraging immigration by promising to give not less than a labor of land, 177 acres, to each farmer, and not less than one sitio or league, 4428 acres, to each stock raiser.

This law also made it clear that there was to be no "buying or selling of slaves, and all children born of slaves in the empire were to be freed at fourteen years of age." This colonization law of 1823 also required the settlers to be Catholic if they wanted the Mexican nation to protect them.

And the new country, the new free land for William Goyens, continued to grow. The scenery in and around Nacogdoches was especially beautiful and inviting and reminded Goyens greatly of his beautiful North Carolina. Benjamin Lunday, the famous abolitionist, in his diary of the 1800s, gave a description of the landscape very similar to the one Goyens had listed in his diaries. Goyens chose to live in the rich setting as a resident of the struggling Nacogdoches community. Leaving the discriminatory regulations of the southern United States, he had come to the crossroads of Texas pioneer activity, the town of Nacogdoches.

William Goyens' fame as a scholar steadily grew in Nacogdoches. He was a hospitable man with a steady traffic of learned guests in his home. "In Nacog-

26

doches there are five or six men," wrote a close friend of Goyens, "who are acute scholars in both tongues, Spanish and English, and Goyens is one of these." Circumstances which had surrounded his birth and early life reflected Goyens' times and the need for the reform so that men could be truly free whether they were black or white. Goyens' literary skill and productivity won him fame and the patronage and esteem of the great, in what was to become Texas.

Unlike many of his Negro friends, he was aware of the true significance of freedom and the tremendous changes it was to bring. He became the most important leader of his race and, because of his ceaseless and unbounding energy and the existing conditions, he was to be a great liberator who never broke with his Anglo friends. He followed the revolts of labor by slaves throughout the southern part of the United States, and he was appalled by the bigotry and the intolerance of the leaders. But Goyens was a man who possessed a great dislike for the weakness of egotism and vanity. He was brilliant and discerning and maintained that strength of character so essential to leaders in the early days of Texas.

In his early life, he became a blacksmith, and the 1828 census listed this as his occupation. His shop was crude with only the floors and the four walls to contain his work. He was honest and fair in all of his dealings and worked many long and late hours. The sweat would pour from the tall Negro as he worked in his humble surroundings. His spirit was never weak, and he gained the esteem of all who knew and worked with him. People in the area knew that William Goyens was a servant not only of mankind,

27

but a servant of God. He prospered greatly and soon worked as a gunsmith.

In this, too, he became an expert and in the year 1831, though he was still single, became a Roman Catholic and worked with the Mexican leaders. This he did to comply with the Mexican colonization law of 1823 which encouraged all settlers in Texas to be of Roman Catholic faith.

When some of his friends were around, they enjoyed the generous hospitality that was extended to each individual who came in contact with William Goyens. "You must be Goyens or no one," cried a visitor who came into town, for he heard of the kindness of this individual. His path soon crossed with many more great men who would eventually help him in his climb to fame as a free Negro. He grew in stature, and became a prominent businessman in a time when it was unheard of for a free Negro to own property.

In the year 1832, William Goyens married the beautiful Mary Sibley, who was originally from Georgia and the widowed mother of Henry Sibley. He was a good provider, a good husband, and because of this became more prosperous and expanded his businesses in the early 1830s. His basic source of wealth was his blacksmith shop in which he worked slaves as well as hired white men, because there were a few slaves in Texas at that time. He made guns for the Spanish and the Mexicans as well as Anglos who desired these, and Goyens was constantly buying, selling and trading land. He was active in civic life and many times aided law enforcement officers in tracing down criminals including those of his own race. He was a genius in law and was frequently involved in court litigation in connection with his varied business

28

His basic source of wealth was his blacksmith shop.

and social activities, and his interest in politics is illustrated by his active role in a campaign for the election of an alcalde in Nacogdoches on September 1, 1824.

Because he was gifted with the desire to serve humanity, he also manufactured wagons and carried on a very successful trading business hauling freight between Natchitoches, Louisiana, and Nacogdoches. Throughout his years in his beautiful East Texas town, Goyens borrowed, loaned and traded money and goods of all kinds. There were many who were unscrupulous and tried to take advantage of him during these years, and sometimes these controversies ended in court.

On one particular occasion of May 7, 1826, Goyens bought a lot in Nacogdoches from Pierre Mayniel for seventy pesos. Today the Nacogdoches County Courthouse stands on this property. It was on this lot located near the present courthouse that Goyens built a home and operated a hostelry. This added to an unusual accumulation of property by this great and enterprising Negro. By 1832, William Goyens had acquired title to acreage about four miles west from Nacogdoches on El Camino Real. It was here that he built a two-story home on a hill just off the road. Today residents of Nacogdoches and the area call this hill Goyens Hill. As one sees it today, there is a church near the top named the Goyens Hill Baptist Church. Approximately fifty miles west at the Goyens homesite just off El Camino Real, there are springs that flow the year around. Residents of the area say that Goyens kept a sort of wayside lodging house which was known far and wide as a very hospitable resting place.

In the records of Blake, we find that Goyens owned

2,000 acres in one ranch and ran a sawmill and grist-mill. One can still look today and see the remains of a dam that William Goyens built on the Ysleta Creek approximately one mile south of his home. This is probably the site of the gristmill. His wealth and his acreage fluctuated considerably from year to year, and because he was an honest and industrious individual, he acquired much wealth. He soon owned 3,818 acres of land in Nacogdoches County and 9,056 acres in Houston, Cherokee and Angelina counties.

He never tried to hide his color and all records of the man indicated that he never once tried to pass as a white man, for in his heart he believed that all men are created equal, and that they should have the same opportunities in this country. It was the great Erasmo Seguin who once commented that this was a great free man who accepted a man for what he was, regardless of the color of his skin.

Though the times were hard, especially in this lawless, adventurous frontier, William Goyens accepted the challenges and the trials of his age. There were no law enforcement agencies in the 1820s and early 1830s that would protect Goyens, and at times he had to resort to buying his freedom. An unscrupulous individual whose name was Yangles promised to release Goyens for 1,000 pesos, and to accumulate that sum, Goyens sold part of his property and exchanged others to gain his freedom. Learning of the situation, another individual enslaved Goyens and was to take him to New Orleans to be sold, but William Goyens was not to be outdone and petitioned the Alcalde of Nacogdoches stating that he was a free man and intended to remain free. This request cleared the situation, and Goyens was never threatened again with the horrible thought of his enslavement. The accounts here listed that Goyens walked to a corner of his little shop, kicked rubbish off some boxes, and in one of them got the required amount. The master wrote a receipt in full and took the money and left town on the next stage.

One day as Goyens sat in his office, a gentleman walked in and, without looking up from his writing, Goyens requested the man to be seated. The man had attempted to collect money for ownership of William Goyens but left without further pressing the issue. Many years of friendship and his crucible of literary achievement heightened the admiration of the people for William Goyens. They knew him as a man in a common experience who was delighted to live life for its maximum benefits. No one was aware of all of Goyens' accomplishments, and many did not know the tremendous amount of land that the free Negro owned in East Texas. Many felt that he had a likeness similar to Alexander the Great or Achilles.

During those trying and formative years, Goyens felt that no individual is free from defects of human frailties. From his boyhood he had tried to improve on his manners so that he would not be slighted by the Anglo. He liked to dress simply, did not wear the fancy garments of his day, but was an ordinary individual though he possessed considerable wealth. A friend wrote, "He seemed to be born and made for friendship, of which he is the sincerest and most persistent individual. Neither is he afraid of that multiplicity of friends who accept only rich individuals. Accessible to every tender of intimacy, he is by no means choosy in his acquaintance while he is most accommodating in keeping it on foot, constant in retaining it. If he has fallen in with anyone whose faults he cannot cure, he finds some opportunity of parting with him, untying the knot of intimacy without tearing it; but when he has found any sincere friends, whose characters are suited to his own, he is so delighted with their society and conversation, that he seems to find in these a chief pleasure of life, having an absolute distaste for individuals who are insincere in all of their dealings. It should be added that, while he is somewhat neglectful of his own interests, no one takes more pains in attending to the concern of his friends. What more need I say? If anyone requires a perfect example of his true friendship, it is in William Goyens that he will best find it.

"In company his extraordinary kindness, sweetness of temper, are such as to cheer the dullest of spirit, in alleviating the annoyance in the most trying circumstances. In boyhood, as I knew him, he was always so pleased with a joke that it might seem that jesting was the main object of his life; but with all that, he did not go so far as buffoonery, nor had ever any inclination to bitterness. From quite a youth, he wrote farces and acted them. Indeed, he was the individual of whom we were all proud. There is nothing that occurs in human life, from which he did not seek to extract some pleasure, although the matter may be serious in itself. If he has to do with the learned and intelligent, he is delighted with their cleverness; if it is unlearned and stupid people, he finds amusement in their folly. He is not offended even by the most ignorant individuals as he adapts himself with marvelous dexterity to the tastes of all, and even his wife finds him humorous and playful." These were the kinds of comments that one would hear in Nacogdoches.

And another wrote, "His house seems to have a sort of fatal felicity, no one having lived in it without being advanced to higher fortune, and no inmate having ever had a stain upon his character. It would be difficult to find anyone living on such terms as did William Goyens. His character is entirely free from any touch of avarice. He has set aside out of his property what he thinks sufficient for his livelihood, and spends the rest in liberal fashion. While he is still dependent upon his occupation, he gives every client true and friendly counsel with an eye for their advantage rather than his own, generally advising them the cheapest thing they can do is to come to terms with any and all opponents." When he could not persuade them to do this, he pointed out how they might be able to get results in the frontier Texas.

It was always part of his character to be most obliging to everybody in his blacksmith shop, his gunsmith shop, and in all of his land dealings. He was very conscious of the individual and of doing good to others. William Goyens counted it a great gain to himself if he could relieve some oppressed person and make a difficult path clear for one who seemed to fall into disgrace. No one more readily conferred the benefit, no man expected less in return, and successful as he was in so may ways, he never offended a mortal being on purpose. He placed his fellowman so far above his own needs and desires. This man found a home in Texas and, because of this, was proud of his new heritage in a land which offered so much opportunity. Such was Goyens in Nacogdoches in the 1820s and 1830s, and today there are still people who can recall a little of what William Goyens left for his fellow beings.

5

ONCE WILLIAM GOYENS
was certain that the way of the Texans was for him,
he readily applied himself to aiding Texas in whatever
way that he could and turned his attention to public
affairs. His close friend, Juan José Sanchez, who was
a witness to his marriage to the lovely Mary Sibley,
was a frequent visitor of William Goyens. Like Father
Deus, the Roman Catholic priests in Nacogdoches at
that time were all frequent visitors. Goyens was active
in civic life and in the campaign of Encarnacion Chirino for Alcalde of Nacogdoches, he tried to rally and
strengthen himself and others to support the man he
felt most likely to represent the people of the Nacogdoches area. William Goyens spoke with the audacity
of youth, the brilliance of a natural orator, and the

logic of an adept practitioner of the law. His words stirred the hearts of his friends in the Nacogdoches area and their courage mounted, but they did reject the man whom Goyens had selected, Chirino.

Goyens' scholarship and his desire for even more knowledge was surprising during those early years in Texas. He had a working knowledge of law, his theology was better than that of many in orders, astronomy fascinated him, and he knew the science of geometry. He read Thomas Aquinas with the same ease that he could compose a tune or fashion a horseshoe in his blacksmith shop.

William Goyens had applied himself wholeheartedly to business and transactions of all types. Success came with remarkable quickness and soon he was the recipient of an annual income, according to the books, that exceeded the income of many wealthy landowners. It is difficult to judge the worth of money from one age to the next, but one may hazard the estimate that Goyens' income compared with the modern standards of approximately $15,000 per year.

So great were the demands upon him that there was at one time no man in East Texas more important in general counsel. His hours were crowded, yet he found time to work with the leaders in political arenas and a judicial office of no small importance. Goyens performed the duties of his office extremely well, and he held it with high honor. He was careful, but quick in his decisions, and many times individuals would come to him for advice. He was just, he had wide knowledge of the law, and often when the litigants were poor, he omitted the fee due him.

The care and skill and wisdom which Goyens displayed as an early Texan did much to win him the esteem and popularity of his fellow citizens, and it also gave him a valuable and profound schooling in human nature. Success in this endeavor was matched by domestic tranquility. The little misunderstandings between the bride and groom, the scholar and the country miss, had vanished, and his wife now had the understanding of her husband's bent and was not afraid of his distinguished friends. She was a devoted lady and offered aid to her husband in every way.

Because Goyens was a Negro, his life was affected in many ways by various circumstances. He often faced the hazard of his heritage, the possibility that some white man in a lawless time might try to take advantage of his race or might try to force him into servitude. Goyens' every hour was apportioned to a duty or a task, and he was impatient with unimportant matters that diverted him or took his time. He thought he was neglecting his reason for living in many of these times.

In a letter to his friend, Sam Houston, he complained, ". . . for while in pleading and hearing and deciding causes, or working in the blacksmith shop or running the grist mill, in waiting on some men about business, and on others out of respect, the greatest part of the day is spent on other men's affairs. The remainder of it must be given to my family at home so that I can reserve no part to myself, that is, to study. I must gossip with my wife and chat with my children and find something to say to my friends. For all these things I reckon a part of my business unless I were to become a stranger in my house, for with whatsoever either nature or choice or chance has engaged a man in any relation of life, he must endeavor to make himself as acceptable to them as he possibly can. In such occupations as these, days and months and years slip away. Indeed, all the time which I can gain to myself is that which I steal from my sleep and my meals, and because that is not much, I have made but a slow progress.''

He made no mention of the long hours he gave to his personal religious freedom. Each morning he would pray. Each day this busy man recited prayers and read the Psalms with his household. He made numerous pilgrimages and, in the interest of self-discipline, he studied the Bible whenever there was an opportunity. Always he tried to maintain discipline over his self-being.

". . . for while in pleading and hearing and deciding causes . . . the greatest part of the day is spent on other men's affairs. . . ."

6

THESE WERE TURBULENT YEARS in the early days of the territory that was later to become the Republic of Texas. Almost fifteen years had elapsed between the planning of American settlements in Texas and the time when she would win her independence. William Goyens saw the Mexicans and the Americans living at peace with one another with little thought of revolution. But now there was ample evidence that William Goyens' good friend, Stephen F. Austin, and many of the early settlers, who had come to Texas with the intention of becoming good citizens of Mexico, were discouraged.

In a letter Goyens stated, "As is the case with most uprisings, I see two groups of causes responsible for a possible revolution in Texas. There are underlying

41

or basic causes which prevent the friendship of the two peoples from being as wholehearted as it might have been and, from time to time, these underlying differences are emphasized by encounters between Anglo-American and Mexican officials. It is from this point forward that Anglo-Americans in Texas, plus such other groups as occasionally join with them in opposition to the Mexican government, will soon be called Texans."

William Goyens understood the underlying causes of the revolution better than most Texans at that time. Because he belonged to a minority group, he knew the feelings on both sides. Chief among these underlying causes was the great difference which existed in the cultural and political traditions of the two peoples. The blunt, self-assertive nature of the American frontiersman was in marked contrast to the more subtle nature of the Mexican. Men such as Jim Bowie and Goyens' personal friend, Sam Houston, were quite different from the Mexicans who lived in the territory that was later to become Texas.

The Texan, being the personification of individualism, had little respect for tradition and could never understand the Mexican's reverence for authority. The heritage of one called for freedom of religion while that of the other demanded reverence for the established Catholic church. Goyens recalled that one made a god of trial by jury while the other found little merit in the system. The Texans' interpretation of local self-government was hopelessly at odds with the varying interpretations of the wholly unstable central government in Mexico.

Goyens further noted that another difficulty arose

42

from the ownership of slaves by Texans while the policy of the Mexican government was one of opposition to slavery. Although this issue never resulted in violent action, it was beyond a doubt a cause of worry and dissatisfaction. This situation bothered Goyens many times although he was a free Negro.

William Goyens noted that there were problems of government and also much to criticize in the government at that time. The Texans were in general satisfied with their local government, especially in Nacogdoches and much of East Texas, as it was entirely in their own hands. The state government, on the other hand, was far less pleasing.

Most of the people of the states of Coahuila and Texas were Mexican and lived in Coahuila. Goyens knew that from the mathematical point of view it was more than fair that these Mexicans of Coahuila control both the legislature and the government in the territory that was later to be known as Texas. The Texans, who were permitted only two members of the legislature to Coahuila's ten, thought, in fact, that they were unrepresented and William Goyens agreed with this philosophy. Although the Texans' representation was later increased to three members, Goyens saw that the attitude toward the government underwent little, if any change.

Of still greater importance, and probably the most important as William Goyens saw the situation, was the unsatisfactory court system. The courts were an abomination to the Texans. Conditions were made worse because the Mexican government was never able to trust completely the American residents of Texas. Goyens himself was never really trusted by the Mexican government because he was an educated man, one who understood people whether they were black or white. Mexico feared her progressive neighbor to the north, and repeated efforts of the United States to acquire Texas caused Mexico to suspect the motives of the Americans living in Texas.

William Goyens was under constant surveillance while at work in his blacksmith shop or in his home. Goyens noted in his diary in the early years in Texas this statement, "There was a complete lack of understanding between the two peoples. I see that both Texans and Mexicans are proud of their heritage and culture, language, religion and tradition. The Texans, however, look with open contempt upon Mexican culture and, worse still, upon the Mexicans themselves. I find this attitude on the part of the Texans to lead to only one course of events. Attempts to enforce the law will meet with opposition, opposition will lead to armed encounters, and armed encounters will lead to revolution."

Later in Texas history, this is what happened. The underlying differences were too great to overcome. They caused minor encounters to be magnified out of all proportion to their importance, and led Texas inevitably along the road to revolution. It later became necessary to examine some of the incidents which led finally to war and the loss by Mexico of a great and wealthy portion of her empire.

William Goyens had just arrived in Texas when one of the first encounters between Texan and Mexican troops occurred. The clash is dignified by the name of the Fredonian Rebellion, but it did not involve enough people to justify the name. A casual acquaintance of Goyens was one of the contract seekers who descended upon the state in 1825. The man

44

was Haden Edwards who had already spent three years in Mexico City watching the uncertain course of Mexican politics.

Haden Edwards, in due time, was given a contract by the state which authorized him to settle 800 families in the eastern portion of Texas, including the area around Nacogdoches. Edwards reached Nacogdoches, as Goyens recalls, in September, 1825 and found a respectable number of families, both Mexican and American, living nearby. Edwards' contract required that he respect the holdings of all settlers who had proper titles to land, and this he was doubtless prepared to do.

William Goyens did not have title to his lands as was the case of numerous Mexican families living in the area who had never completed their titles, even though in some instances their families had occupied the same land for a century. The American squatters, none of whom had legal rights to the land, also had limited titles as did the Cherokee Indians. Edwards made unsuccessful attempts to collect fees from some of Austin's colonies who had settled east of the San Jacinto and who had titles properly issued. All of these individuals petitioned the Mexican authorities in San Antonio and the Governor of Saltillo to revoke the Edwards grant.

William Goyens worked night and day helping write letters and trying to help his fellowmen in Nacogdoches in whatever manner possible. He was careful not to oppose Edwards openly for he would have jeopardized the very freedom he had in Texas. Edwards and his brother were unwilling to accept the fact that they would be ordered out of the country. As a result they quickly made an agreement with agents of the Cherokees calling for a division of the land between Americans and Indians. On December 16, 1826 a small band of men led by Benjamin Edwards rode into Nacogdoches and proclaimed the Republic of Fredonia.

These were frightening days, but William Goyens drew himself up and, with all of the pride and dignity of the great individual that he was, lent courage to many of his fellowmen in Nacogdoches. When Edwards and his men rode into Nacogdoches that day, they established themselves in a building known as the Old Stone Fort and unfurled a red and white flag bearing the words Independence, Liberty and Justice.

William Goyens noted that, in spite of the name, the flag, and the motto, this episode was not an example of an appreciable group of people seeking independence, liberty, and justice for at this time, the Fredonians numbered not more than fifteen men. At no time did as many as thirty men adhere to the program. Goyens, who later was to become the chief negotiator for Sam Houston with the Cherokee Indians, found that the Cherokee alliance was worthless, and the agents who had negotiated the agreement were executed by the Indians themselves.

The rebellion received no support from the other settlements, and the anticipated aid from the United States did not materialize. In describing the incident at a later date to a close friend, Goyens said, "The venture can best be described as an exercise in futility." Tempers raged in Nacogdoches during this period and on January 22, 1827, before the arrival of the troops and militia which were sent from Stephen F. Austin, the Fredonians gave up the farce and most of them crossed the Sabine into the United States.

"The Fredonian movement and venture can be described as an exercise in futility."

William Goyens knew even too well that, though it was a small rebellion to justify, the Fredonian movement had far-reaching effects. It convinced many Mexicans that the Americans were not to be trusted. These Americans, as Goyens had stated many times, were a proud and a free people. Goyens visited with his friend Seguin and found that it was the feeling of the Mexican people that the United States ultimately wanted to either purchase Texas or take her by force.

The revolution was brewing there in East Texas and throughout the Texas soil. Mexico had become more and more doubtful of the wisdom of permitting Americans to settle in Texas and, as a result of the uprising, a garrison of two hundred men was established in Nacogdoches in June, 1827. Goyens in a letter stated that the commanding officer, Mariano Coso, was succeeded in September of 1827 by Colonel Piedras. Goyens, like many of the settlers, looked with some distrust upon the establishment of this garrison in peaceful Nacogdoches, but as time went on, they forgot their fears.

Each day in beautiful East Texas towns, many immigrants of the United States continued to arrive in large numbers. The year 1829 was an eventful year for William Goyens as in the fall, the Texans were notified by President Guerrero that slavery was abolished in Mexico. The Mexican officials in Texas believed the move to be unwise, so did not publish the decree. Goyens, through personal contacts and friends, however, found this decree and kept a copy in his possession. The Mexican officials urged modification of this new policy arguing that the slaves had been legally acquired and that granting them freedom in this manner would do their owners a great injustice.

William Goyens, because he was a Negro, kept quiet in all of these matters. He listened to the Texans and to the Mexican officials as they argued that this would create a severe economic hardship if the decree were enforced, and that trouble with the colonists in Texas might result. Goyens, with several of his friends, secured copies of the decree and presented it to many of the people in East Texas. The colonies, after learning of the decree, became very excited. This came to nothing when it was learned that Guerrero had taken the advice of his subordinates in Texas and had exempted the province from the provisions of the decree.

Guerrero in Goyens' opinion, however, did make one concession for in the statement he made, he clearly indicated that no more slaves could be introduced into Texas. In making this statement, he was merely repeating a provision of the state constitution which Goyens had memorized. The colonists had long since learned to evade bringing in their slaves as contract servants. This was a method that many had used to bring in slaves throughout the state.

The interpretation, which robbed the decree of its effectiveness in Texas, quieted the colonies, but it did not remove a fear which had developed in the minds of many, the fear that perhaps one purpose of the president had been to discourage immigration from the United States. Even the East Texans, who were only slightly worried by the president's decree, were thunderstruck by a law passed the following year which was known as the law of April 6, 1830. In many respects, this act marks the turning point in the relations between Mexico and her American colonies.

William Goyens felt that it would not be long before the revolution would come, and with the fighting, freedom would come at some point in the future. Goyens would long remember the day of April 6, 1830, for the law that was passed. This law grew out of a report made by Gen. Manuel de Mier y Teran who had been sent to Texas in 1828 on a tour of inspection.

Teran was definitely worried because he found in Texas ten times as many Americans as Mexicans. To make matters worse, he found that most of the Mexicans in Texas were very poor and uneducated. Teran was convinced that Mexico was undoubtedly in danger of losing Texas, and he made a number of suggestions intended to improve the Mexican position on the province. In these suggestions, William Goyens could see that his people would be aided to a great extent.

In order to increase the Mexican population in Texas, Teran proposed a colonization project to be sponsored by the Mexican government. Under this program, poor families would be transported to Texas at government expense and convict soldiers were to be given lands after completing their terms of service in the army.

As another means of offsetting the numerical superiority of the Americans, Teran thought that the government should attempt to attract Swiss and Mexican immigrants to Texas. As further guarantees of Mexican supremacy, he proposed that the number of troops in Texas be considerably increased and several new military posts be established. Also, he hoped to bind the province more tightly to the mother country by developing economic ties through the encouragement of coastwide trade.

This was a tremendous plan, Goyens thought, for

the Mexicans once again to gain control of Texas and the surrounding area. Goyens knew, however, that the actions of the controlling bodies in Mexico would be slow, that possibly revolution would come about before any of these plans could be implemented. One provision was implemented, however, for the garrisons of San Antonio, Goliad, and Nacogdoches were strengthened, and new garrisons were established at these places: Tenoxtitlan on the Brazos, Anahuac on Galveston Bay, Lipantitlan on the Nueces, Teran on the Nueces, Lavaca on the Lavaca, and Velasco near the mouth of the Brazos. The colonists and Goyens soon realized that they were surrounded by a ring of troops, and no one liked that situation.

In 1832 at Anahuac, trouble had developed. The commander there, John Davis Bradburn, an American soldier of fortune from Kentucky, proved to be particularly unpopular. Bradburn was impressed by the dignity of his position and failed to use tact in dealing with settlers. Land titles were not predominant then, and Bradburn tried to seize land which did not have a title.

Francisco Madero was sent to the area with authority to issue land titles, but Bradburn questioned Madero's authority and ordered his arrest. This zone was placed under martial law, as Goyens recalled. The settlers were angry, but were not provoked to violence, and there matters rested for some months.

Meanwhile, attention was shifted to George Fisher, another American in Mexican service. Fisher arrived in Galveston to take over his duties as collector of the port. Before he could get his office in order and begin collecting taxes, General Teran issued an order postponing the establishment of a customshouse. Fisher, who had a good command of both Spanish and English, was then sent to San Felipe as an interpreter. Fisher set up his own agency collecting tariffs and soon was in trouble with the colonies. In trying to settle the differences that existed between Texan and Mexican alike, Teran acted wisely in removing him.

Bradburn, however, continued to needle everyone and was despised by Goyens. He angered Goyens by his attitude, by using slave labor in the construction of military buildings without compensating their owners, and by pressing for supplies for his garrison. The worst action was the arrest of certain popular citizens.

Patrick C. Jack, who had organized a militia company, found himself in Bradburn's guardhouse as a result. William Barret Travis, who attempted to obtain the release to their owner of two slaves whom Bradburn had enlisted in his force, promptly became a companion of Jack in the guardhouse. The friendship of Travis and Goyens grew, for Travis believed in individual rights. It was not long before Bradburn resigned and made his way to Louisiana, and Juan Cortina was placed in command at Anahuac. These were some of many such incidents witnessed by Goyens in East Texas during the early 1830s.

In Mexico, Gen. Antonio Lopez de Santa Anna's revolution against the Mexican president, Gen. Anastasio Bustamante, was taking place. Eventually Santa Anna was to win, but Bustamante had many loyal followers in East Texas and especially in Nacogdoches. East Texans basically resented the presence of Mexican forces and Goyens knew violence would soon follow.

On August 2, 1832 a group of angry colonists led

52

by Col. James W. Bullock entered Nacogdoches. To Goyens' amazement, they immediately attacked a garrison of Mexican forces which Col. Don Jose de las Piedras commanded. The battle began but the Mexican forces, realizing they needed protection, retreated to an old stone fort in the heart of Nacogdoches. William Goyens did not get involved for this was a personal matter between the colonists and Colonel Piedras.

On August 4, 1832 Colonel Piedras, realizing that the fighting was futile, surrendered his company to the Texans. Goyens was present at the Durst House on the banks of the beautiful Angelina River west of Nacogdoches when the surrender occurred. This battle was later called the Battle of Nacogdoches.

Tempers mellowed with peace and order restored in the town of Nacogdoches. Goyens worked in his blacksmith shop servicing those needy individuals in all walks of life. Several days after the Battle of Nacogdoches, Goyens was surprised to see Colonel Piedras. The colonel called on William Goyens to forge two large cans with lids out of two large copper pots. Goyens worked hard trying to accommodate the colonel to the best of his ability. His large muscular arms grew somewhat tired, however, in trying to form the cans in a manner that would accommodate everything that was to be placed in them.

After Goyens had completed this work, Colonel Piedras dismissed him for his job was finished. The next day, however, William Goyens was again summoned by Colonel Piedras for another task. Goyens did not understand what this task would be, for he had worked long and hard on the two large cans and felt that his job had been completed. On arriving before the colonel, Goyens was called inside. The colonel instructed Goyens to seal the cans, but he also instructed him not to look inside.

Goyens went about his work and sealed the cans pretending not to see what was inside. That night as he returned to his home, he wrote in his diary the events of that day. "On this day I have worked for Colonel Piedras of the Mexican army, and I have sealed two large containers approximately four feet high and two feet in diameter with Mexican silver and gold pieces. As far as I know, these gold pieces are recent tax collections from the people of this area. In a portion of the other can, there are jewels of various kinds and valuables from the church. In trying to seal these properly, I have soldered the lids on the cans. Somehow I feel that Piedras is anticipating some sort of battle for he has given specific instructions to his men as to what they are to do with these containers."

A few days after the battle, Goyens received information that the large containers were buried on the banks of the Ysleta Creek. Piedras was captured before he could recover the treasure and, according to Goyens, it was never found.

Goyens soon met another friend, an abolitionist, Benjamin Lundy. Goyens was neutral during these years because he knew the problems of the Negro and especially the free Negro. Because he was a large businessman and had a large home, Goyens found it necessary to own slaves himself. The 1830 census indicated that he owned three slaves, but that he was buying and selling before that date.

On January 3, 1829 he purchased a twenty-six year-old male slave named Jerry from John Durst for seven hundred pesos. The same year Goyens and Elijah

A few days after the Battle of Nacogdoches, Colonel Piedras buried the two sealed containers on the banks of the Ysleta Creek.

Loyd both claimed a slave woman and her six or seven children, all of whom were formerly owned by Susan Calier. The case went to court and the verdict was handed down on September 30, 1829 in favor of Elijah Loyd.

On November 6, 1829 Goyens bought a Negro named Sally, age thirty-five years, and her six-year-old daughter, Luisa, from Susan Calier. That same year, one of Goyens' slaves, Jake, was involved in poisoning a family. The family recovered, and Jake was severely punished by Goyens. It was Benjamin Lundy who gave some insight into Goyens' private life for he recorded this in his journal.

Lundy, who was an American abolitionist, dreamed of forming a colony in Mexico near the town of Tamaulipas. On two of these trips, he passed through Nacogdoches and each time visited with William Goyens.

Lundy admired Goyens because Goyens was a free Negro who understood not only the free Negro's position, but the position of the slave as well. In Lundy's journal of his second trip through Nacogdoches, he discussed the stay he had with Goyens in the Goyens home. He commented on Goyens and his wife and their life together as he saw it. This document was recorded in Lundy's journal on July 14, 1834:

"I went about four miles into the country to the house of William Goyens, a very respectable coloured man, with whom I became acquainted here in 1832. He still takes a deep interest in my enterprise. He has a . . . wife who is a native of Georgia. They appear to live happily together, are quite wealthy, and are considered very respectable by the people generally. Goyens has undertaken to procure me a horse, and I am arranging my baggage so as to pursue my journey on horseback." Lundy indicated that he had been in Nacogdoches at an earlier date and had contacted Goyens.

In the diary on July 19, Lundy again noted, "A ball was given tonight by some of the Mexican residents of Nacogdoches. Among the earliest dancers was William Goyens, the coloured man before mentioned. Afterwards some of our Northern Americans joined in the dance. The ladies were all Mexican. Two brothers of the wife of William Goyens . . . have been here about a week having come to visit her from Louisiana where they reside. They appear well satisfied with their brother-in-law whom they had not seen before, and they took a very friendly leave of the family today." Apparently Mrs. Goyens was not at the dance on that nineteenth day of July in 1832. Due to Lundy's ideas concerning the free Negro, his views may have been prejudiced or slanted in the direction Lundy would have his reader follow.

But Lundy was to leave and needed a horse. Goyens, looking about, soon procured a Cherokee pony so that his friend Lundy would be able to travel on. As Lundy was leaving, and as he travelled on horseback, he recalled the friendly, hospitable William Goyens who did everything possible to aid him in support of the abolitionist's dream for the free Negro.

Goyens lay awake that night dreaming of the day when all men would be free and his race would be able to walk with the Anglo and the Mexican shoulder to shoulder in this country, so that each of them would have the same opportunities afforded the other. Goyens spent a sleepless night visualizing the many things that needed to be done for the Negro people, for the slaves, and for all the oppressed.

57

7

No MAN IS AN ISLAND,
and William Goyens, although strong in many ways,
was no island. Those years from 1834 to 1836 are
years well remembered in Texas history. Stephen F.
Austin, the patient man and Father of Texas, tried
desperately to settle with the relentless Mexican authorities. Many times his requests were unheeded.

William Goyens found the Texans in a state of
great excitement although they had been quiet during
most of the time he had been in early Texas. There
was no real need of excitement in 1833 for the people
had held their conventions, and William Goyens listened while many had listed grievances and had petitioned for redress. The reforms granted by the federal
and state governments of Mexico satisfied all but the

most radical Texans and, for a time, discontent was largely banished from the province.

Col. Juan Almonte, an agent sent to study conditions in Texas, reported to the government in 1834 that Texas was peaceful and would remain so, and political order could be established in the Mexican province. It seems, however, according to William Goyens' knowledge, that political stability was beyond the power of the Mexican government at this time and, in 1835, difficulties developed anew.

During these times, neither service to the state nor the Mexican government, nor the traffic of many guests prevented William Goyens from supervising in detail the training of his children. The household was a testing ground for his theories of education and love for mankind. Here was taught and lived the Christian belief that in a perfect society there would be two authorities, the natural and the supernatural, and that the latter, being God's will, should govern the first. This is what Goyens taught in his home and it was the rule by which he lived; it was the principle by which he died.

His good wife tried valiantly to follow the conversations of her husband and his guests, and the equally high talk of the children's learning. Although it was sometimes confusing, she understood the aims of William Goyens' program. Not meant to be a student herself, she adopted the rule and role of a stern headmistress and supplied her own lack by keeping a watchful eye on the children. Hours of study were rigid and were enforced, and there was little malingering or evasion under the rule of the wife.

Goyens knew in these trying years that a dictator can brook no opposition, and Santa Anna planned an immediate showdown with the Texans. Fever was high in Nacogdoches in opposition to Santa Anna. This was the feeling throughout Texas among the Negro, the Mexican, and the Anglo. General Cos was ordered to lead an army into Texas and establish himself in San Antonio.

Meanwhile, the Texans were choosing their delegates to the consultation. Stephen F. Austin, writing for the San Felipe Committee of Correspondence, urged the people to select their representatives with care. The people of Nacogdoches, after considering the many residents in the area who were qualified, decided to select William Goyens. Goyens debated a long time before refusing to go to the consultation, for he felt that he would be discriminated against at such a large consultation where tempers would be on edge.

The consultation, which was scheduled to meet in San Felipe on October 6, 1835, had a rude awakening. Two weeks before that date and one week before the arrival of Cos in San Antonio, both Mexican and Texan were brought face to face with cold reality by an unexpected clash at Gonzales, the Lexington of Texas. The people of Gonzales had a brass cannon which had been given to them four years before for use in fighting off Indian attacks. It was these same Indians who had made William Goyens a negotiator of treaties.

William Goyens received several appointments, during those early years in Texas, to act as an interpreter in Indian affairs for the Mexicans and Texas, as it was not unusual for Negroes on the Texas frontier to be closely associated with Indians. A thorough treatment of this relationship may be found in many places in early Texas history. Goyens was chosen as negotiator primarily because he was born in an area of the country which was in close proximity to the area in North Carolina occupied by the Cherokee Indians.

Most of the Indians involved in the negotiations in Texas were the Cherokees and their associated bands. The Texas Cherokees had once been a part of the great Cherokee nation which was scattered around the southern Appalachian area and was a formidable part of the Indian population in America numbering at one time approximately 20,000 people. The Cherokee Indians in Texas were a band that had moved from an area of North Carolina, Tennessee, and northern Georgia to Texas by way of Arkansas arriving there in the winter of 1819 and 1820. They established their homes, as did Goyens, in eastern Texas. Some ventured near the Angelina, Neches, and Trinity rivers. They were a small group in number, but were joined by remnants of the Delaware, Shawnee, Kickapoo, Quapaw, Choctaw, Biloxi, Iawanie, Alabama, and Coushatta Indians. This entire nation of tribes became known as the Cherokee and their associated bands and here William Goyens had worked to bring peace between the red man and the white man although he himself was a black man. The associated bands followed the lead of the Cherokees, since the Cherokees formed the largest and most important contingent. These Indians were dependent mainly on agriculture, and it was important that they have some claim to the land which they occupied.

Chief Richard Fields of the Cherokees attempted to obtain rights to their land from the Spanish government, but was not successful due to the government upheavals in Mexico. It was during the negotia-

62

Chief Richard Fields of the Cherokees attempted to obtain rights to their land from the Spanish Government, but was not successful . . .

tions between the Mexicans and the Spaniards that William Goyens acted as an interpreter for the Mexicans. His participation in Mexican-Indian relations was indicated in a letter written by Chief Fields to the Alcalde of Nacogdoches on August 26, 1826. Fields had proclaimed allegiance to the Mexican government believing that Mexico had approved the Indian land claims. Thus, he must have felt compelled to ask the alcalde for permission to wage war against the Wacoes, the Comanches, and the Tahuacanoes.

Goyens brought Fields' letter to the alcalde in which Fields stated, "I, Richard Fields, First Captain of the Cherokee Nation, and in its name represent to you that all my people came to me and insisted, for reasons that I found well-grounded, that I apply to you to give us leave, if you have the authority to do so, to go to war with the hostile Indian Nations such as the Wacoes and the Comanches who have killed some of our people and enraged us to see them committing daily outrages upon our Coahuila Texas fathers. . . . Indeed, we consider ourselves sons of the Mexicans, and we cheerfully offer our persons and the last drop of our blood for the defense of the country. . . . My people were disposed to take the authority in their own hands, as I informed you in a previous letter. Three sons whom you sent to me, Louis Procela, William Goyens, and Nathaniel Norris, will bear testimony to the disposition. Evidence from our men and those of other nations on whose assistance I can rely will be given as soon as they are established here."

Almost a decade later, Goyens served as an Indian agent for the Texans. In 1835, the Texans, actively involved in gaining their independence especially from the Mexicans, feared a possible Indian-Mexican coalition. It was here that William Goyens took an active role in helping the Texans in a just cause. Although the Cherokee and the Mexican possessed no affection for one another, they did share a common animosity toward the United States and to those who had come in and had taken this land which they had once owned. Apparently the Texans attempted to exert some influence among the Indians in the opening period of the struggle for independence, for it was William Goyens who was chosen for the transmission of messages to the Cherokees.

Though there are no records of this early outcome, a letter issued from Thomas J. Rusk to Chief Bowles read as follows: "Your talks have reached us by the hands of your friend, William Goyens. . . . We have heard that you wish Mr. Goyens to go with you and hear the talk on the Brazos. We are willing that he should go, because we believe him to be a man who will not tell a lie either for the white man or the red man."

The Texas consultation which met at San Felipe de Austin November 3, 1835, passed a declaration providing for a provisional government for Texas. The declaration reflected the Texans' concern in the matter of Indian-Mexican togetherness when it arranged for the general council and the governor to have the power to negotiate with the powerful Cherokee Indians of East Texas and especially Nacogdoches. The consultation wanted the negotiators to establish definite boundaries for the Indian land, giving the Indians a claim to the land in exchange for their agreement to remain at peace during the revolution.

A portion of the declaration referred to the Indians read as follows: "We solemnly declare that it is our sincere desire that the Cherokee Indians and their associated bands shall remain our friends in peace and war, and if they do so, we pledge the foregoing declarations. We solemnly declare that they are entitled to the protection as the just owners of the soil, as an unfortunate race of people that we wish to hold as friends and treat with justice from henceforth."

Goyens' friend, Sam Houston, was one of the individuals appointed to treat with the Indians. Another good friend, John Forbes, also accepted an appointment to meet in February, 1836. Goyens accompanied Houston and Forbes to the meeting of the Cherokees and interpreted all messages between the Indians and the great Sam Houston. The Houston-Forbes Treaty was negotiated and signed setting the boundaries for the Indian land as northwest of El Camino Real, the old San Antonio Road, and between the Sabine and Angelina rivers. The treaty promised this land to the Indians if they remained in peace during the Texas Revolution.

On December 20, 1836, after Sam Houston was elected president of the new Republic, the treaty was sent by Houston to the senate for ratification where it met stiff opposition, and then was referred to a standing committee on Indian Affairs with no favorable results. Houston was anxious to maintain contact, and called upon his friend, William Goyens, to serve in the capacity of Indian agent. This was a position of great importance since the fate of the struggling Republic demanded conditions of internal comprehensiveness. The presence of Mexican agents among the Cherokees necessitated a counterbalancing influence, and Goyens proved to be a valuable link between the Texans and the Cherokees.

In writing to Goyens, Sam Houston wrote, "My dear friend, be so kind as to write to me all the news, and I wish you to cure Colonel Bowles' eyes. Give my respect to Mr. Bowles, agent, and tell him how much I rely upon him. Tell him to write me often."

In the warlike attacks from the Indians during the early periods of the Republic, there was no evidence to show that the Cherokees were involved. In fact, they took a neutral stand and many times tried to bring peace to the border, because they respected Sam Houston and Goyens, who acted as an agent for procuring all necessary items and propositions in the treaty itself. Bowles, Houston's counterpart, made several trips to the frontier in trying to maintain the Houston-Forbes Treaty, and it was Goyens who procured the provisions for Bowles' trips. Many bills signed by Goyens, as the acting agent, indicated that he accompanied Bowles at least as far as the Grand Saline Creek. Goyens was very conscientious and wanted to work and serve in the best capacity that he could.

One of his letters written on a late night indicated the following: "General Sam Houston, Sir: During the week last past, first week in May, 1837, I was notified by Bowles of his return and of his wish that I should attend a talk at his village on Saturday last. Pursuant to this invitation, together with Colonel Millard, I arrived at Bowles' town at the appointed time. A council was formed and Bowles communicated in a speech, without any variation, the same that he had already narrated to Colonel Millard and myself. The substance of his speech in relation to his journey is as follows:

"After his departure from the village, he proceeded to the upper waters of the Trinity where he found the Caddoes to whom he made a speech. Bowles was not happy with the report he heard from one of his scouts on his arrival that the whites had talked of suspecting him of an intention to form a league with the Indians against Texas. He had satisfied himself with the reflection that no white man of standing would form such an opinion, but only the very dregs of the people would do so.

"I had once requested him not to mention it in council, but to continue to repose his confidence where he always had placed it and where it never could be misplaced, in General Sam Houston and in me. With this, he was perfectly satisfied and complied with my desire accordingly. The council was about to break up. Big Mush rose, and in the most urgent manner, requested that all that had transpired in the council should be commemorated verbatim without omitting anything. He stated that you thus far had endeavored to comply with the request faithfully and hoped it would prove satisfactory. I have the honor to be with respect, Your obedient humble servant, William Goyens."

At the bottom of the letter were the following remarks: "I have examined with care the foregoing statement of Mr. Goyens and, finding it circumstantially correct, it will be unnecessary for me to report as I can add nothing to it. Henry Millard."

General Houston used this letter in trying to get passage of the law by Congress authorizing the use of the supposedly peaceful northern Indians in operations against the most hostile prairie Indians. In a letter from Sam Houston written in the city of Houston on

Goyens had worked to bring peace between the red man and the white man, although he was a black man.

June 7, 1837, he made the following remarks: "Get the Cherokees, Shawnees, Biloxis, Kickapoos and Coushattas and Choctaws to go out if possible with policies that have been made. Everything must be done for the protection of the frontier and to chastise those murderous hordes of wild Indians. See Goyens and say that I will write very soon and to do all in his power to forward matters. General Sam Houston."

In another letter dated a few weeks later from the city of Houston on June 16, 1837, Houston again remarked, "General Rusk, I wish you to notify Mr. William Goyens, the Cherokees, the Shawnees, the Delawares, the Kickapoos, through any media that you may deem best that I wish to meet their chief at Nacogdoches on the 30th of this month. We must act as far as possible to aid our country. I wish to get out the corps of mounted gunmen so as to secure the frontier with the aid of friendly Indians."

After the successful meeting, Houston wrote a letter to the Bowl, chief of the Cherokees, July 3, 1837, Nacogdoches, Texas. "Brother, I wish to see you at this place in four days. I wish you to send word to Big Mush and bring him with the other chiefs. I wish you to send word to the Kickapoos, and if the Caddoes will come down or send three chiefs as well as the same number of Kickapoo chiefs, they will be well treated, and I will take them by the hand. I wish things to be done soon. I will be happy to see you and my brothers. I want you to bring the copy of the treaty which I last sent to you. It has a ribbon and a seal on it. I am very anxious to see you. You must tell my sisters and brothers that I have not forgot them, that they live in my heart. Sam Houston."

The following day, another letter to William

"Colonel Bowl, Chief of the Cherokees, I wish to see you in Nacogdoches in four days. . . . You may tell my sisters and brothers that I have not forgot them, that they live in my heart." Sam Houston, July 3, 1837

Goyens from Gen. Sam Houston read as follows: "Mr. William Goyens, Agent, Sir: I send on the same letter a letter to my brother Bowl, and would be glad if you could take it to him and have it examined and brought down with the other chiefs. Let word be sent to the other tribes as directed. If you do not go, see that the letter goes as soon as you can return. I will only have a short time to stay in this place. If you see Colonel Bean, tell him that I am anxious to see him here. Give my compliments to your family. Your friend, Sam Houston."

All of the groundwork had been laid, and now the senate was to debate on the issue of the treaty. Goyens had done his job, for he had brought the red man and the white man together with the great friend of the Indians, Sam Houston. Goyens' friendship with the Cherokee was conveyed in the treaty, but over the objections of General Houston, the treaty was declared null and void on December 16, 1837 by the Texas Senate. With all of these unanticipated happenings, the defeat greatly disappointed Sam Houston, but he continued in his attempt to satisfy the Indian land claims as outlined in the treaty negotiated by William Goyens.

The lawmakers of Texas, after viewing Goyens' work, were greatly disturbed by Houston's actions in this respect and, in rejecting the treaty a second time, made it quite clear that they were against granting land to Cherokees. Much to William Goyens' disappointment, there was evidence of public support to show that the Cherokees were conspiring with the Mexicans. The evidence was there to support the existence of such a coalition. Don Pedro Julian Miracle and Vicente Cordova, former Alcalde of Nacogdoches, entered Texas on May 29, 1838 with an armed expedition consisting of approximately seventy-two persons, including Mexican soldiers and Cherokee Indians. Miracle died near the Red River on August 20, and on his body were found letters which were proof of the coalition of the Cherokees and Mexicans.

Gen. Thomas J. Rusk soon received reports of the movements of Mexicans among the Indians. Rusk, who was in constant communication with Houston during the incident, tried to bring harmony to the Indian people. Rusk again turned to the most able man in Indian negotiations, William Goyens.

Rusk made the following statement: "I have just heard from the spies I sent out this morning as an escort to Goyens who carried my letter to Bowles, a copy of which you have. They left Goyens at Lacey's." This probably referred to Martin Lacey's home near the Angelina River. Rusk continued, "He said he and Leonard Williams would go to Bowles tonight."

On a bright sunshiny morning, Goyens reported to Rusk on the meeting with Bowles, for on the fifteenth, Rusk wrote to the chief indicating that he had received reports, and that he wished to make a peaceful arrangement with him. With all of the knowledge and wisdom that he had acquired during the years, Goyens sat back, ready to serve in whatever capacity that his good friend Houston and Rusk would have him serve.

The letter from Rusk read, "My friends, Colonel Bowles and Big Mush, Chiefs of the Cherokees: I have received your talk about Durst and also your talks about Goyens with all of which I am well pleased. I want no difficulties with your people or,

73

in fact, with any of our red brethren who have been my friends. The Mexicans have lied to you and have lied to us in order to raise trouble between us. They are not after any good to us or you, but after benefits to themselves.

"We have talked to you before; what I have said stands. Let it stand unbroken between us. You may rest assured upon the word of a warrior who has never forfeited that word that no harm shall come to you or your women and children. Your women and children are frightened, but they have nothing to fear from our warriors in the field in different parts, but you may assure your people there is no danger to them. All we want is to chastise our enemy, the Mexicans, or force them to lay down their arms and surrender themselves to the laws.

"Your cornfields shall not be disturbed or any of your property injured, and if we buy anything from you, it shall be paid for. Goyens and the agent are authorized to talk to you fully. Appoint any place and we will come and talk to you. Any of your men can come in perfect safety with Durst or Goyens to headquarters where I would be pleased to see any of you. There is no cause for trouble or misunderstanding between you and our people. Your friend, Thomas J. Rusk."

While the crisis continued, Mirabeau B. Lamar succeeded Gen. Sam Houston on December 10, 1838 as president of the Republic of Texas. His policy had not changed toward the Cherokees, for he, unlike Houston, despised the Indian. He did not feel that they had any right to the Texas land and wanted them out completely. Lamar had visions of an empire that stretched from the Pacific Ocean to the Gulf of Mexico, and no Indian had any part in his dream.

When the Indians did not move, Lamar ordered the Texas army, under Secretary of War Albert Sydney Johnston, to move against the Cherokees that fateful July 17, 1839. Though the Indians were defeated, they were never forgotten. Goyens hung his head, for he had served as an Indian agent under the great Sam Houston, but he could not desert his Cherokee brethren. As the sun set that day in 1839, Goyens was saddened, for his many years of work were destroyed when Lamar ordered the Texans to drive the Cherokee from their beloved homeland.

8

IN THE YEAR 1841, Goyens was a familiar figure throughout the Nacogdoches territory. He was constantly buying, selling, trading, doing whatever he possibly could to earn dollars in the part of the country where color was finally laid aside. The courts proved to be grounds where Goyens made constant appearances.

Arguments over land ownership was a continuous occurrence in early Texas, and such a disagreement brought Goyens into court for an 1841 session. Over 1,000 acres on Posskins Creek, southeast of Nacogdoches, proved to be quite troublesome for William Goyens during that year. It was Stephen J. Stanley who conveyed the land to Goyens in the spring of

1841, and Goyens claimed that Stanley had resold the land to another individual, James Beard.

Goyens lost his case and was assessed $30.50 in court costs. He went home that night, unsatisfied but not beaten, for Goyens knew in his heart that he was right. The following morning he filed suit against Beard and on May 11, 1841, lost his claim again. He paid the court costs of $32.53. Because he was a determined man, and since he knew he was right, he decided in November to try again on this particular section of land, but he lost again.

Throughout his court involvements, Goyens distinguished himself among his fellowmen in Nacogdoches. His ability and understanding of the benefits and the restrictions incurred in the laws surprised everyone who witnessed any of the trials. The years would pass, and Texas was soon to become a state in the United States of America. During the early years of the establishment of the Republic of Texas, the Anglos restricted the passage and immigration of free Negroes into Texas. The ordinance did, however, grant citizenship to those free Negroes who were then living in the Republic.

The constitution of 1836 required all free Negroes to secure congressional approval to remain in the Republic. This constitutional prohibition was lifted in June, 1837 by house and senate joint resolution which read: "For the relief of all free Africans or descendants of Africans who are residing within the Republic at the adoption of the Constitution, resolved by the Senate and House of Representatives of the Republic of Texas, in Congress assembled, that all free Africans or descendants of Africans who were residing within the Republic of Texas at the time of the adoption of

Arguments over land ownership was a continuous occurrence in early Texas, and such a disagreement brought Goyens into court for an 1841 session.

the Constitution are hereby granted and allowed the privilege of remaining in any part of the Republic as long as they choose on the condition of performing all the duties required of them by law."

Goyens realized that this would not last long, and in February of 1840, another portion was added. "Section 8. Be it further enacted that two years shall be allowed from and after the passage of this act to all free persons of color, who are now in this Republic, to remove out of the same and all those who shall be found here after that time, without the permission of Congress, shall be arrested and sold as provided in this Act."

Goyens was saddened again, for this would mean giving up twenty years of work and the property that he had accumulated. It would mean leaving friends and the area which he loved so much, for East Texas, with its beautiful sumac in the fall and autumn, the tall pines which were green throughout the year, all brought a sense of freedom to William Goyens.

His dear friend, Thomas J. Rusk, drew up a petition asking permission for Goyens to stay in Texas. Signing the petition were fifty-four citizens of Nacogdoches, and some of the most prominent names throughout the area were listed on this. These included Rusk, Adolphus Sterne, Charles Taylor, Bennett Black and others.

The contents read, "The petition of the undersigned would respectfully represent unto your honor bodies that William Goyens, a free man of color, has resided in the county of Nacogdoches for a number of years past and has conducted himself as an honest, industrious citizen, has accumulated considerable property and lands, and has been of great service to the country in our Indian difficulties. Your petitioners believe that it would be an act of justice and would with great respect solicit of your honorable bodies to pass an Act authorizing the said William Goyens to reside permanently in the Republic and enjoy such privileges as are usual in like cases and your petitioner will ever pray. September, 1840."

William Goyens spent many sleepless nights awaiting the outcome and the verdict on this particular petition. His friends all wished him well, and as he journeyed through Nacogdoches, he would visit with each of them during these perilous times. It was not long, however, before congress approved the petition on November 25, 1840.

A little over two weeks after the approval of Goyens' petition, on December 12, 1840, congress passed an act allowing some free Negroes to remain in Texas. It read, "For the relief of certain free persons, all free persons of color, together with their families who were residing in Texas on the day of the Declaration of Independence, are and shall be exempt from the operation or provisions of an Act of Congress approved 5th of February 1840, granted permission to remain in this Republic."

Goyens was very happy with the verdict, for his friend, Sam Houston, issued a similar proclamation on February 5, 1842 permitting the Negroes to remain in Texas for the next twelve months. Goyens later tried to secure a league of land which was rightfully his for having served the Republic of Texas, and for having lived here the many years. His first appeals were rejected, but this was not enough to prevent Goyens from seeking justice in this matter.

After Texas joined the United States, he tried

again, and the senate listened to a petition and referred it to the Committee on Private Land Claims. It read as follows, "It appears from evidence that Goyens is a free colored man, that he resided in Nacogdoches County as early as the year 1824, that he was a married man and, under the laws of Mexico, was entitled to a headright of land for one league and one labor, that he did in the year 1835 obtain from the then authorities an order for survey, but from the fact of his being appointed by General Houston, then commanding the forces of Texas, interpreter for the purpose of restraining hostilities by the Cherokee Indians which appointment General Rusk states he filled with much credit to himself. It also appears that he, Goyens, served in the Army of Texas during her dark hours of the revolution shoulder to shoulder with the white man. The premises considered, the committee has determined to report for the consideration of this Senate a bill for his relief, all of which is submitted."

He never gained the land, because of a motion by Senator M. D. K. Taylor of Titus and Cass counties to table the bill. No further action was ever taken. (See appendix) Goyens had all the qualifications for obtaining the land, all the qualifications except one: he did not have white parents.

Throughout the period of independence, most Texans were eager to have the Republic become a state in the United States. The aim of the revolution had been not so much to gain independence as to obtain an American form of government. It was generally realized that it would be difficult for a country with so small a population to retain its independence and to meet the expenses of government. Most Texans, and William Goyens was no different, were convinced that annexation to some larger and wealthier country offered the best solution to the majority of their problems. Most of the Texans, including Goyens, who had lived in the United States and were familiar with its political and social traditions, found it natural to turn their attention to that country.

In the election of September, 1836 the Texans voted almost unanimously in favor of annexation. Houston's first minister to the United States, William H. Wharton, carried with him a proposal that Texas should become a part of the larger republic. Wharton obtained the recognition for the Republic of Texas, but it was 1845 before Texas was finally annexed.

Texas developed so rapidly during the fifteen years between annexation and secession that a casual observer might conclude that the state inherited none of the problems of the Republic. William Goyens was the first to admit that such a conclusion would be incorrect, for he knew that insofar as physical conditions were concerned, annexation had few magic properties.

In the first winter of statehood, the sun was no brighter and the northers were no less biting than any other winters. The Indians raided the frontier settlements of the state as freely as they had raided the frontier settlements of the Republic. The debt remained as great a problem as ever, yet annexation did bring important changes.

Goyens noted in one of his diaries that Texas no longer faced the problem of maintaining a position among the states of the world. It was no longer necessary to send and receive diplomatic agents, nor was the state called upon to maintain an army and navy. The average citizen had greater peace of mind and a greater feeling of security than he had experienced for years.

There was a feeling of satisfaction in the knowledge that something long desired had been acquired at last.

Most Texans were happy at the turn events had taken, but the few who had dreamed of a Republic extending to the Pacific found little cause for exultation. As these men sat before their fires during the long winter evenings, they no doubt saw in the dancing flames visions of what might have been had Texas followed another route.

Annexation, as Goyens recalled, placed Texas a slave state in the midst of the American slavery controversy. For some years the slavery question remained threatening in the background, but as time went on, it became more acute and, in the end, it was instrumental in forcing Texas and ten of her sister states from the union.

It was during the decade of the 1850s that the slavery issue reached a critical stage. The status of the free Negro became increasingly precarious, and conditions in the recently admitted slave state of Texas were certainly no exception. Discrimination was here in the white population as it was elsewhere. In the census of 1850, there were 397 free Negroes listed.

William Goyens and his lovely wife did not live to see the final outcome of the slavery question for each died in 1856. When the controversy was at its highest over the Kansas personal liberty laws, Mary Sibley Goyens died in February of 1856. William Goyens had lost his faithful wife who helped him so many times through the years. It was a simple burial on the hill that was later to be called Goyens' Hill where Mrs. Goyens was laid to rest in a plain box coffin. Goyens grieved deeply.

It was not long until William Goyens became ill

at his home in June of that same year. He had been active in business as late as January seventeenth, for then he had sold over 100 acres of land near the Alazan Creek to Alexander Meyers for a sum of $1.50 per acre.

Dr. William Tubbe visited with William Goyens for three days and four nights before the final breath came on June 20, 1856. William Goyens, the great Negro man, was buried beside his wife near a large cedar tree on Moral Creek in a Mexican cemetery approximately three miles from his home.

It was not until 1936 that the State of Texas, sensing Goyens' historical significance, placed a historical marker on his grave.

With the death of his stepson, Henry Sibley, in March of 1849, and Mary Goyens' death in February 1856, the only heirs to the estate were Henry Sibley's two daughters, Henrietta and Martha. The day after Goyens' death Henry C. Hancock, a Nacogdoches lawyer, requested the court to appoint him administrator of Goyens' estate. The court granted the request, called for an inventory and appraisal of the Goyens property. The appraisal was filed on August 19, 1856.

At his death Goyens owned 12,423 acres of land with 3,887 acres in various tracts located in several grants west of Nacogdoches near Goyens' Hill. The largest single tract of land was 4,428 acres in Angelina County, originally granted to Anastacio Barrella. The estimate of his wealth in the year 1856 was $11,917.60.

The marker has many mistakes, but it does at last give recognition to a man who had come from a background in North Carolina which did not approve of many liberties or privileges for free Negroes. He had come to Texas using his talents and intelligence to build a life which held something more. He started from a simple and humble beginning. He had a blacksmith shop, and he was friendly to all people regardless of race, creed, or color. He was fair and dealt with people in terms of themselves as individuals, for this was the way he wanted to be treated. William Goyens never once had any delusions of being inferior or superior to any individual. The grave seems to say something to us today: "His skin was black; his heart, true blue."

Bibliography

Austin State Library, *Memorial No. 13, Original Petition*

Barker, Eugene, Amelia Williams, *The Writings of Sam Houston*

Blake, Ed., *Census Reports, Eastern Texas*

Blake, Robert, *Blake Collection, Historic Nacogdoches, Research Collection, Texas Census Records, William Goyens, Locations of Spanish Missions.*

Burke, Edmund, *Eulogy of James Fox*

De Bow, J. D. B., *The Seventh Census of the United States*

Franklin, *The Free Negro in North Carolina*

Franklin, John Hope, *From Slavery to Freedom*

Gammel, H. P. N., *The Laws of Texas*

Lundy, *The Life, Travels and Opinions of Benjamin Lundy*

Maurcier, Davie, *Negroes in American Society*

Millard, Henry, *Telegraph and Texas Register*

Nacogdoches Archives *XXX*, 59

Nardini, Louis Raphael, *No Man's Land, The History of El Camino Real*

Oldham, Williamson S., and George White, *A Digest of The General Statute Laws of The State of Texas*

Porter, Kenneth, *Negroes and Indians on The Texas Frontier*

Prince, Diane Elizabeth, Thesis *William Goyens*

Rusk, Thomas, *Thomas J. Rusk Papers*

Smither, Harriet, *Diary of Adolphus Stern, Southwestern Historical Quarterly*

Stamp, Kenneth, *The Peculiar Institution*

Tillery, Edwin, *With Writer, Nacogdoches, Texas*

White, George W. and Williamson Oldham, *A Digest of The General Statute of The State of Texas*

Williams, Amelia and Eugene Barker, *The Writings of Sam Houston*

Wolfolk, *"Turner's Safety Valve and Free Negro Westward Migration"*

Worthham, *A History of Texas*

Yoakum, *History of Texas*

Appendix

JOURNAL

of

THE SENATE

of

THE STATE OF TEXAS

FOURTH LEGISLATURE

———

PUBLISHED BY AUTHORITY

———

AUSTIN

PRINTED BY CUSHNEY & HAMPTON,

"STATE GAZETTE" OFFICE

1852

Page 340   Monday, January 19, 1852.

The Senate was called to order by the President pursuant to adjournment — prayer by the Rev. Mr. Smith — roll called — quorum present.

The Journal of Saturday was read and adopted.

Mr. Truit presented the petition of Charles B. Slaughter; referred to the committee on Private Land Claims;

Mr. Sterne presented the petition of W. W. Barrett; referred to the committee on Private Land Claims.

Mr. Taylor, chairman of the committee on Private Land Claims, reported back to the Senate, a bill for the relief of the heirs of John Norman, deceased; and a bill for the relief of Andrew Roach, and recommended their passage.

Mr. Taylor made the following report:

The committee on Private Land Claims, to whom was referred the petition of William Goynes, have duly considered the same.

It appears from the evidence that Goynes is a free colored man, that he resided in Nacogdoches county as early as the year 1824, that he was a married man, and under the laws of Mexico was entitled to a headright of land for one league and one labor — that he did in the year 1835, obtain from the then authorities, an order for survey for said quantum of land, and would have had the same secured by survey, but from the fact of his being appointed by Gen. Houston, then commanding the forces of Texas, interpreter for the purpose of restraining hostilities by the Cherokee Indians, which appointment, Gen. Rusk states, he filled with much credit to himself. It also appears that he, Goynes, served in the army of Texas during her dark hours of the revolution, shoulder to shoulder with the white man. The premises considered, the committee have determined to report for the consideration of the Senate, a bill for his relief. All of which is submitted.

A bill for the relief of William Goynes; read first time.

* * * * *

Mr. Davis introduced joint resolution relative to the location of the various tribes of Indians within the limits of Texas; read first time.

On motion of Mr. Reaves, Mr. Eddy was added to the committee on Engrossed Bills.

* * * * *

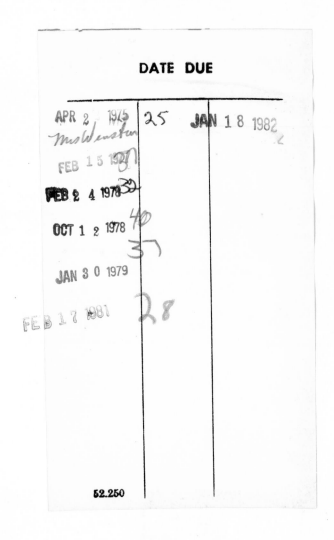

DATE DUE

APR 2 1975	25	JAN 1 8 1982
Ms Weinstein		
FEB 1 5 1977		
FEB 2 4 1978		
OCT 1 2 1978	40	
	37	
JAN 3 0 1979		
FEB 1 7 1981	28	

52.250